Cambridge English Readers

Starter Level

Series editor: Philip Prowse

The Black Pearls

Richard MacAndrew

CAMBRIDGE
UNIVERSITY PRESS

LONGWOOD PUBLIC LIBRARY

CAMBRIDGE UNIVERSITY PRESS

Cambridge, New York, Melbourne, Madrid, Cape Town, Singapore, São Paulo, Delhi

Cambridge University Press
The Edinburgh Building, Cambridge CB2 8RU, UK

www.cambridge.org
Information on this title: www.cambridge.org/9780521732895

© Cambridge University Press 2008

This book is in copyright. Subject to statutory exception
and to the provisions of relevant collective licensing agreements,
no reproduction of any part may take place without
the written permission of Cambridge University Press.

First published 2008

Richard MacAndrew has asserted his right to be identified as the Author of the Work in
accordance with the Copyright, Design and Patents Act 1988.

Printed in Italy by L.E.G.O S.p.A

Illustrations by Tom Croft

A catalogue record of this book is available from the British Library.

ISBN-13 978-0-521-73289-5 paperback
ISBN-13 978-0-521-73290-1 paperback plus audio CD

No character in this work is based on any person living or dead.
Any resemblance to an actual person or situation is purely accidental.

Contents

People in the story

Janet Hunter
is a police inspector
from New Zealand.

Tunui Epati
is an inspector in the
Cook Islands police.

Wolfgang Peters
is a man who
steals things.

Kate Watson
is a Hollywood
film star.

Maria Gomez
is in a film with
Kate Watson.

Places in the story

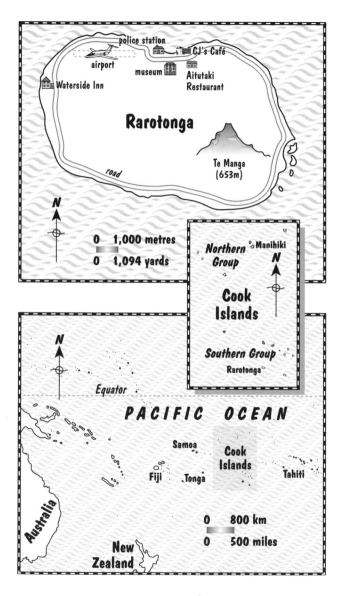

Chapter 1   *Who is Wolfgang Peters?*

'This is the man,' says Janet Hunter, and she puts a photo on the table. Janet Hunter is a police inspector from New Zealand. She's in the police station on Rarotonga, one of the Cook Islands in the Pacific Ocean.

'What's his name?' asks Tunui Epati. Epati is an inspector in the Cook Islands police.

'His name is Wolfgang Peters,' she answers. 'Some people call him the "Minute Man".'

'Why?' Epati asks.

'Because one minute he's there and the next minute he's not,' answers Hunter.

Epati smiles.

'And why do you want him?' Epati asks. He looks at the photo.

'He steals,' answers Hunter. 'He takes things – often from museums. People tell him what they want. Then he steals for them. And he gets very good money for his work.'

'What kind of things does he take?' asks Epati.

'Anything,' answers Hunter. 'A Fabergé egg from a museum in Virginia in the United States, a Picasso painting from a museum in St Petersburg in Russia. And then this year an old book from a museum in Auckland in New Zealand. It's the only one in the world. That's why I'm after him.'

'I see,' says Epati.

'Peters is very good,' says Hunter. 'But I want him. And I'm going to get him.'

'And he's coming here – to Rarotonga?' asks Epati.

'Yes,' says Hunter. 'We, the New Zealand police, think he's going to steal something here.'

'Ah,' says Epati. 'Then I know what – I think.'

Epati takes down a book and opens it. Hunter watches him. Many Cook Islanders are big people; Epati is big.

He gives Hunter the book. It's open at a photo of a beautiful necklace of black pearls.

'That is the Manihiki Necklace,' says Epati. 'It's from the island of Manihiki. Manihiki is a thousand kilometres from Rarotonga, but it's one of the Cook Islands too.'

Hunter looks at the necklace.

'It's beautiful,' she says.

The Manihiki Necklace
Manihiki, 1891

'Yes,' says Epati, 'and over a hundred years old. Those are black pearls. They're not easy to find. You only get them in Tahiti and here in the Cook Islands.'

Hunter looks up at Epati.

'The necklace is in the museum here,' says Epati. 'People from all over the world come to see it.' He takes the photo of Peters from the table.

'Can I have this photo?' he asks.

'Of course,' answers Hunter. Then she says, 'Peters is coming here this morning on a plane from Tahiti. I want to watch him, and try and get him. But is that OK with you? After all, this is your island.'

'That's OK,' says Epati. 'Do you want any help? We have some good people in the Cook Islands police.'

'Thank you,' says Hunter, 'but not now. I can call you.'

'Of course,' says Epati. 'Call me by five o'clock.'

'OK,' says Hunter.

They go out of the police station.

'Which hotel are you in?' asks Epati.

'The Waterside Inn,' answers Hunter.

'Good hotel,' says Epati. 'Is this your first time in the Cook Islands?'

'Yes,' says Hunter. 'It's very beautiful here. Well, thank you for your help, Inspector. I must get to the airport by eleven o'clock.'

Chapter 2 *Watching Peters*

A lot of people are waiting in front of the airport.

'What are all these people doing?' thinks Hunter.

She walks across and speaks to a Cook Islands woman.

'Why's everyone here?' she asks.

'Kate Watson is coming,' the woman answers. 'You know, *the* Kate Watson. She's in a lot of Hollywood films.'

'Oh, her,' says Hunter. 'Is she making a film here?' she asks.

'Yes, but she's only on the island for two or three days.'

Hunter waits next to the woman for a minute or two. Then she goes to her car.

At about 11.45 Wolfgang Peters comes out of the airport. He's a short man with dark hair. Hunter watches from her car. Peters finds a taxi and gets in. The taxi drives away. Hunter drives behind it.

After fifteen minutes the taxi stops at the Waterside Inn and Peters gets out with his bags.

'That's good,' thinks Hunter. 'He's at this hotel too. It's going to be easy to watch him.'

She sits in her car across the street and waits.

At 1.30 Peters comes out of the hotel. A taxi is waiting. Peters gets in and the taxi drives away.

Hunter is behind them.

Peters' taxi takes him to the museum. He gets out and walks into the museum. Hunter leaves her car and goes in too.

The museum is small. There are a lot of interesting things from the Cook Islands, and from Tahiti, Tonga and Fiji. Hunter looks at some old bags and jackets from the Cook Islands. But she watches Peters too.

He's looking at the Manihiki Necklace. After a minute or two he looks across the room. Hunter turns and walks over to a boat from the time of Captain Cook. She doesn't want Peters to see her. Peters looks at the necklace again. Then he leaves the museum.

Hunter waits five minutes. Then she too leaves and goes to the Waterside Inn.

Chapter 3   *At CJ's Café*

'Peters is here,' says Hunter. It's six o'clock in the evening. She's sitting with Tunui Epati at CJ's Café. They're looking out over the water. 'And he *is* going to steal the Manihiki Necklace.'

'Well,' says Epati. 'We can stop him – I can get some police officers to watch the necklace all the time. Or…we can try and get him with the necklace.'

'I want to get him with the necklace,' says Hunter. 'But it's not going to be easy. He *is* very good at his job.'

'I can put some police officers in the museum,' says Epati, 'where Peters can't see them.'

'You can,' says Hunter, 'but …'

'They're not going to get him?' asks Epati.

Hunter smiles. 'The police never do,' she says.

'Well…' says Epati. 'He's at the Waterside Inn. We can look for the necklace in his room.'

'You can try looking in his room too,' says Hunter, 'but he never has the things with him. Virginia, St Petersburg, Auckland – the police never find anything. But ...' She stops and thinks. 'He has a plane ticket to Tahiti the day after tomorrow. And he's not going to leave the necklace here in Rarotonga.'

'No,' Epati says. 'Peters isn't working for a Cook Islander. No-one here has that much money. Peters is going to have the necklace with him at the airport. We can get him there.'

'And no police officers in the museum?' asks Hunter.

'No,' says Epati.

Epati and Hunter leave CJ's Café. Across the street a lot of people are waiting in front of the Aitutaki Restaurant. Some police officers are there too. A car drives up and two

16

women get out. The first has long red hair and is very beautiful. Hunter knows her face from films and papers.

People shout, 'Kate! Kate! How are you, Kate? Do you like Rarotonga, Kate?'

The second woman has dark hair. She's beautiful too. Hunter looks at Epati.

'Who's the woman with dark hair?' she asks.

'Maria Gomez,' answers Epati. 'She's in the Kate Watson film too. She's not famous now, but people say she's the next big thing.'

The women smile and go into the restaurant.

Epati looks at Hunter.

'Hollywood comes to Rarotonga,' he says with a small smile. 'It's all work for me.'

Chapter 4   *Who takes the necklace?*

At nine o'clock the next morning the museum is opening. Hunter is sitting in her car. She's watching the front door of the museum. After five minutes Epati comes out and walks across to her.

'The people at the museum understand,' says Epati. 'They know about Peters and they're not going to try and stop him.'

'OK,' says Hunter.

'Well,' says Epati. 'I'm leaving. We don't want Peters to see any police officers here and I've got work to do. What are you going to do?'

'I'm just going to wait here in the car for now and watch,' says Hunter.

'OK.' Epati gets in his car and drives away.

People come and go in and out of the museum. Then at about eleven thirty, a taxi drives up and a woman with long dark hair gets out. She has a bag in one hand. She looks at Hunter's car and then walks into the museum fast.

Hunter watches the woman. 'Something's wrong!' she thinks. 'I don't think that's a woman!'

She gets out of her car fast. There's a noise from the museum and a lot of shouting. She runs to the museum, but people are running out with their hands over their faces. Hunter tries to get in, but she can't. She runs to the back door. It's open. Two people from the museum come out.

'The necklace,' shouts one. 'It's not there!'

Chapter 5 *Peters knows nothing*

'The "Minute Man",' says Epati.

'Yes,' says Hunter. 'There one minute, not the next. Or this time he's the "Minute Woman".'

It's six o'clock in the evening and they're drinking coconut water at the Waterside Inn.

'What does Peters say?' asks Hunter.

'Nothing,' answers Epati. 'Three hours of questions this afternoon, and no answers from him!'

'He's not the woman at the museum?' asks Hunter. Her mouth smiles, but not her eyes.

'He says not,' says Epati.

'Of course,' says Hunter. 'And what about his room here?'

'No necklace,' says Epati. 'No long dark hair. Nothing.'

'Then why is he in Rarotonga?' asks Hunter. She smiles again.

'He says he's just enjoying our beautiful island,' says Epati. 'Lots of good food and friendly people.'

'Where is he now?' asks Hunter.

'Here, in the restaurant – eating and drinking.' Epati laughs. 'And this evening there's some Cook Islands dancing at the hotel. He's going to watch that because he tells me he loves dancing.'

'He's good,' says Hunter.

'Very good,' says Epati.

Epati looks at Hunter.

'Do you like dancing?' he asks.

'I do now,' she answers. 'I want to watch Peters.'

At nine o'clock Hunter leaves her room and goes down to the restaurant. She hears a lot of noise and shouting.

'Kate! Kate! Are you here for the dancing? Do you like Cook Islands dancing?'

Kate Watson comes into the hotel. Maria Gomez is with her. Hunter walks into the restaurant behind them.

In the restaurant Kate Watson and Maria Gomez sit at the front. Hunter looks for Peters. He is sitting behind Kate Watson.

The dancing starts: men, women, boys and girls all with flowers in their hair – beautiful dances to beautiful music. Everyone enjoys it.

The dancing finishes at 10.30 and everyone gets up to leave. People go to the restaurant doors. Hunter waits and watches. Peters speaks to one or two people. Then he goes to the doors. Watson and Gomez are leaving too. Hunter can just see their heads. Peters is just in front of them. Kate Watson says something to him. He turns and smiles, but says nothing.

People out on the street are shouting, 'Kate! Kate!'

Hunter watches Peters. He turns left to his room. Kate Watson and Maria Gomez go out of the hotel and get into a car.

Chapter 6   *At the airport*

It's ten o'clock in the morning and Hunter and Epati are at the airport. They're watching people. Two planes are leaving this morning: one to Tahiti, one to Los Angeles.

Across the room Hunter sees Kate Watson and Maria Gomez. Someone behind them has their bags. There's a lot of noise. The women are late for their plane. An airport worker looks at their tickets, and then they run to the plane.

After two or three minutes Hunter and Epati see Peters. They run over and stop him.

'Excuse me, Mr Peters,' says Epati. 'Can I look in your bags, please?'

'Of course,' says Peters.

Epati takes the two bags from Peters.

He starts looking in one bag. Hunter takes out Peters' computer and opens it.

'I don't have that necklace, you know,' says Peters to Epati. 'I know nothing about it.'

Epati finishes looking in Peters' bag.

'Nothing here,' he says to Hunter. Then he looks at Peters.

'OK,' he says. 'Put your arms up.' He tries Peters' jacket, his trousers – everywhere.

Hunter watches Peters' face. He doesn't have the necklace – she just knows it. She looks at his computer. 'Is there something here?' she thinks.

Epati turns to Hunter.

'Nothing,' he says again.

Hunter looks up. She thinks for a minute and walks away

from Peters a little. Epati goes with her.

'Peters steals things for people,' says Hunter. 'Then they give him money.'

She looks at Epati. 'Someone wants the Manihiki Necklace. They ask Peters and he steals it for them. He gives them the necklace. They give him the money.'

She starts to speak fast now.

'But how much money?' she asks Epati. '$100,000? $200,000?'

Epati doesn't answer.

'No-one in Rarotonga has that much money. We know that,' she says. Then she puts a hand to her head.

'Of course!' she says. 'Kate Watson.' She looks at Epati.

'Her plane?' she asks. But Epati has his phone out.

'This is Inspector Epati,' he says. 'The plane to Los Angeles must not leave. It must not leave. Get everyone off the plane and into the airport now.'

Epati puts his phone away.

'I'm going to speak to Kate Watson,' he says to Hunter.

'OK,' says Hunter. 'And I'm going to try and find something on this computer.'

Epati goes up to Peters. 'You come with me,' he says.

Chapter 7 *Finding the answers*

At twelve o'clock Epati is sitting in a room at the airport. Peters and Kate Watson are there, and two police officers are next to Watson's bags.

Kate Watson is angry.

'I tell you – I don't know this man. And I don't know anything about a necklace,' she shouts. 'And just look at my bags! You can't leave them like that. I'm not going to forget this, you know.'

Just then the door opens. It's a police officer. He's with Maria Gomez and he has a small bag.

'Excuse me, Inspector,' he says. 'We've got this from the plane. Under Seat 3A – where Ms Gomez is sitting.'

Everyone in the room looks at Maria Gomez.

Her face goes white.

The police officer opens the bag and puts something on the table. The Manihiki Necklace. Everyone looks at it.

'I don't understand...' says Maria Gomez. Her face now goes red. 'I know nothing about this.'

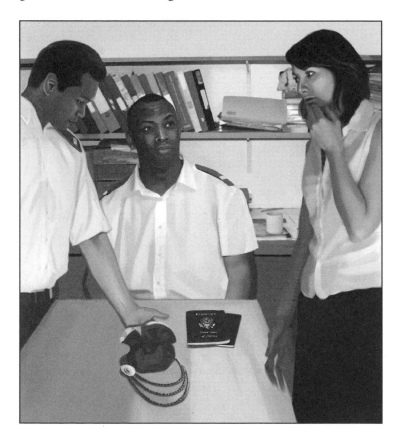

Just then Peters gets up.

'Well, you have your woman, Inspector. I can go now,' he says. But Hunter is by the open door with Peters' computer.

'Sit down, Peters,' she says. 'You're not going anywhere.'

Hunter puts the computer on the table and turns it to Epati.

'Computers are funny things, Peters,' she says. 'It's easy to put something on a computer, but it's never easy to take it off. That email from your bank... not easy for me to find, but very interesting.'

Epati reads the email and smiles.

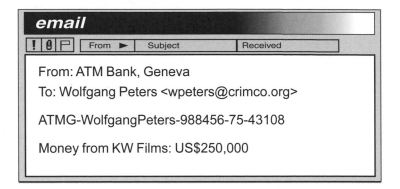

'Thank you, Inspector Hunter,' says Epati. 'That's very good work.'

Hunter looks at Kate Watson.

'And KW Films,' she says. 'Is that Maria Gomez Films? Or is it Kate Watson Films?'

Kate Watson looks across at Peters. Her eyes are dark and angry.

'You stupid man,' she says. 'You stupid, stupid man!'